Portsm

TROLLEYBUSES

Barry Cox

MP Middleton Press

C000052364

Cover picture: No. 294, a 1936 AEC with Craven bodywork, is seen crossing the Guildhall Square en route to the Dockyard on a sunny early summer's evening in 1963. (B.R.Cox)

Dedicated to my late father, Ron Cox - 1915-1998, who was employed as a conductor on the Portsmouth trolleybuses when they were introduced.

Published November 2001
First reprint October 2002

ISBN 1 901706 73 7

© Middleton Press, 2001

Design David Pede

Published by
Middleton Press
Easebourne Lane
Midhurst, West Sussex
GU29 9AZ
Tel: 01730 813169
Fax: 01730 812601

Printed & bound by Biddles Ltd,
Guildford and Kings Lynn

CONTENTS

ACKNOWLEDGEMENTS

I would like to thank, in particular, Tom Dethridge, for the use of many photographs from his extensive collection, also Anthony Triggs for the use of photographs nos. 2 and 93 and *The News*, Portsmouth, for the use of the photograph no. 15. A number of the photographs are also attributable to the late George Tucker, who had the foresight, with many of his views of trolleybuses, as with trams, to depict Portsmouth street scenes, as opposed to the usual close-up views of the subject itself. Other photographs have been attributed where known.

The remaining photographs in the book come from my own collection, but I do acknowledge that these have not all been taken by myself. Where this is the case, and I do not know the actual sources to attribute these photographs to, I hope the individuals concerned will derive the satisfaction of knowing that their photograph has made an invaluable contribution to this publication.

I also acknowledge that I have made use of material contained in, or referred to in, the late S.E.Harrison's definitive book *The Tramways of Portsmouth*, also Milton and Berns' painstaking work entitled *Portsmouth City Transport 1840 to 1977*, Eric Watts' authoritative book entitled *Fares Please* and to an unattributed booklet published by the City of Portsmouth Passenger Transport Department in 1984, entitled *Portsmouth's Trolley Buses 1934–1963 – A Brief History and Fleet List*. Finally, to John Gillham for permission to use his incredibly detailed plan of the system.

I would also wish to express my gratitude to my secretary, Sheila Jones, for all her patience in typing and formatting the material onto disc and for proof-reading and checking this.

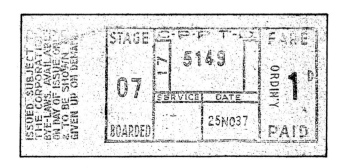

The timetables reproduced herein are from 1958, unless otherwise stated.

INTRODUCTION

I am aware that some readers have expressed the view that a book on Portsmouth trolleybuses has been a long time coming. I hope that all readers will find the wait has been worthwhile.

I am of a generation that can readily recall the Portsmouth trolleybus system during the late fifties until its demise. I have vivid memories of incidents peculiar to trolleybuses like the noise experienced if you were sitting in the upper deck when there was a dewirement of the booms (poles) at a junction. I particularly have recollections of such dewirements at the junction of Chichester Road with both London Road, North End, and Copnor Road. I also recall leaving school in Mayfield Road daily and running to catch the no. 5 from the Monckton Road stop to Copnor Bridge and on occasions having to run to jump on board as the trolleybus sped away – the acceleration really was quite electric! One incident which really remains with me is waiting to cross the road at North End Junction late one afternoon in the summer of 1958, having just been to a matinée at the nearby Odeon, and being shocked when the end of a trolleybus boom from no. 201 landed in the road close to me, following a dewirement – another yard and, well, I would not be compiling this book!

Turning to the system itself, the first trolleybus to run in service in Portsmouth took to the road on 4th August 1934, and the last, on 27th July 1963.

In this publication I have sought to provide an interesting and evocative selection of photographs, the majority of which have never been published previously, covering the complete era of this silent and pollution-free form of transport in Portsmouth. To minimise duplication of views in similar locations I have included sections dealing geographically with routes and not covering each individual route along its entire length. Readers are referred to John Gillham's most detailed plan of the system included, and also to the chronology of routes included, for details of individual routes themselves.

The selection of photographs includes many taken by me between 1961 and 1963 and, where possible, I have tried to show the trolleybuses in street scene settings to enable readers to take a nostalgic trip back to the Portsmouth of comparatively recent bygone years – a city described perhaps somewhat unfairly as a northern city located on the South Coast because of its drabness, and as recently as 1968, by a delegate to the TUC Centenary Conference being held at the Guildhall that year, as resembling an East European city because of its number of derelict sites. I am sure that today's citizens would not share these views!

I hope that you enjoy the journey.

GEOGRAPHICAL SETTING

The geography of Portsmouth is such that it is essentially an island, Portsea Island, with a district, Cosham, extending for about one mile to the north, as far as the slopes of Portsdown Hill.

Portsmouth is also extremely flat, most of it lying no more than a few feet above sea level with the highest point being Fratton Bridge in the centre of the island.

Another main feature of the city is that, until 1941, there was only one bridge providing access to and from it, and that was Portsbridge linking Portsea Island with Cosham. Indeed, the trolleybus system only ever traversed Portsbridge throughout the duration of the system.

On the face of it, the Portsmouth trolleybus system was reasonably straightforward, comprising a compact collection of routes which largely followed the pattern of the former tram routes running north/south from Cosham to Hilsea, just south of Portsbridge, and then along three main roads to termini at the southern end of Portsea Island at South Parade Pier and Clarence Pier, serving the seaside resort of Southsea, and at the Dockyard, which was the industrial heart of the city.

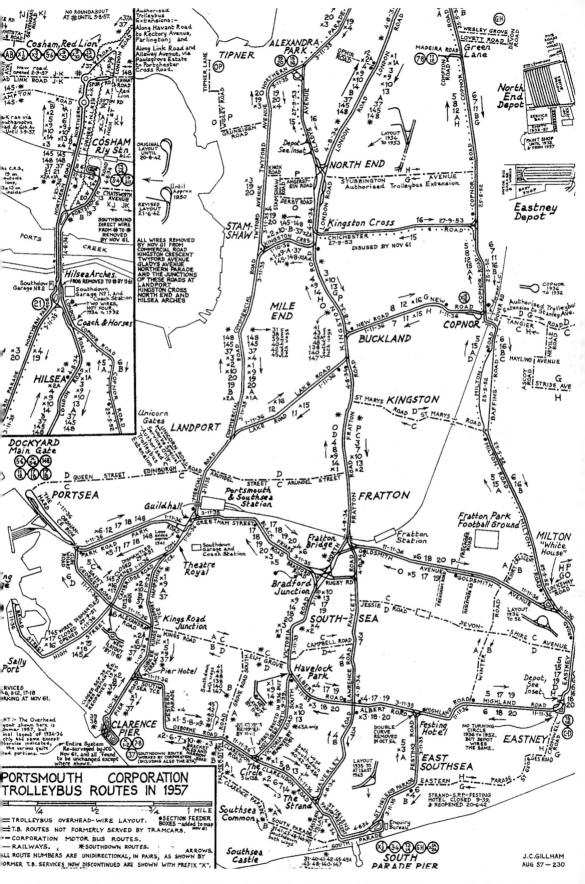

PORTSMOUTH CORPORATION TROLLEYBUS ROUTES IN 1957

TROLLEYBUS OVERHEAD-WIRE LAYOUT.
T.B. ROUTES NOT FORMERLY SERVED BY TRAMCARS.
CORPORATION MOTOR BUS ROUTES.
RAILWAYS.
SOUTHDOWN ROUTES.

SECTION FEEDER BOXES—added to map Nov 61

ALL ROUTE NUMBERS ARE UNIDIRECTIONAL, IN PAIRS, AS SHOWN BY
FORMER T.B. SERVICES NOW DISCONTINUED ARE SHOWN WITH PREFIX "X".   ARROWS.

J.C. GILLHAM
AUG 57 – 230

HISTORICAL BACKGROUND

The decision to convert the tramway system to trolleybuses was taken by the city council in 1933, after members of the Transport Committee had visited several towns and cities in Britain to inspect their trolleybus systems.

Initially, tenders were invited for the supply of 15 experimental trolleybuses and these were accepted in December 1933. Nos. 1 to 11 were 50-seat four-wheelers, and nos. 12 to 15 were 60-seat six-wheelers. These vehicles were quite deliberately varied to enable evaluation of the various types to take place to see which were most suited to local operating conditions.

The first trolleybus service was from South Parade Pier to Cosham and this was officially opened on 4th August 1934, following a Ministry of Transport inspection on 1st August. The departure of no. 14 at 09.05 hours from Cosham Railway Station compound en route to South Parade Pier on route 3-4 took place following an official send-off in the presence of the Chairman and Members of the Tramways Committee, and Mr Ben Hall, the General Manager, and other officials. A ten-minute frequency was maintained all day by trolleybuses nos. 5, 6, 7, 10, 11, 14 and 15.

The rest of the 15 experimental vehicles entered service throughout the remainder of August, and these proved so popular – over one million passengers travelling in the first twelve weeks of operation on the Cosham – South Parade Pier route alone – that the decision was taken by the council to accelerate the abolition of the tramway system.

Following the delivery of a further nine trolleybuses (nos. 16 to 24) towards the end of 1935, trolleybuses were introduced along Commercial Road and to Hilsea via Twyford Avenue. There was a slight delay in this extension because the road under Portsmouth Town Station had to be lowered to give enough headroom for the trolleybuses which were slightly higher than the trams. The erection of wires along Northern Parade from Alexandra Park to Hilsea afforded the opportunity to run the trolleybuses direct to Cosham from Commercial Road and Twyford Avenue, there having been no previous tramway link between these points as Northern Parade was not in fact constructed until the early 1930s, and it was decided not to extend the tramway along

this road in view of the impending decision to abandon the tramway system.

In early 1936, the council decided to convert the rest of the tramway system so tenders were invited and accepted for another 76 four-wheel AEC trolleybuses with English Electric equipment, and bodies by Cravens of Sheffield. These vehicles received the numbers 25 to 100 and were all delivered between August and December 1936, enabling the abandonment of the tramway system to proceed rather more quickly than had originally been intended, with the result that the final trams ran on the 17-18 route on 10th November 1936.

With the outbreak of World War II, all the roofs of the trolleybuses and motorbuses were painted grey to make them less conspicuous from the air. Also the ultimate route destination on the vehicles was not displayed, as an added attempt to confuse the enemy – perhaps somewhat unnecessarily, bearing in mind that any infiltrators would almost certainly have arrived with detailed maps of the area!

Although it was also declared policy to increase trolleybus operation at the expense of motor vehicles in an effort to save fuel, there were still cuts and revisions to services imposed largely as a security measure to protect passengers travelling in vehicles along the sea front area, but also as a cost-saving measure to assist the war effort. These cuts and revisions occurred during July 1940. After hostilities ended, the trolleybus services returned to normal, and indeed from 1st July 1946 new routes and extensions commenced. However, the attractive pre-war livery incorporating white roofs was never reintroduced and grey painted roofs remained through to the close of the system.

The 1950s began with the withdrawal of the 1 and 2 service and also the (original) 15-16 trolleybus service to the Floating Bridge but 1952 saw the extension of the 7-8 and 11-12 routes to Green Lane via Copnor Road, also the extension of the 5-6 service to Cosham 'Red Lion' along Milton Road and Copnor Road and the introduction of a completely new trolleybus service, 15-16 from Alexandra Park to Eastney via Chichester Road, replacing the E-F motorbus service. The day before this service commenced, however, the 9-10 service was temporarily suspended, never in fact to be reintroduced.

During the late 1950s there was considerable debate within the city council as to the future of trolleybus services and, following an independent consultant's report, a decision was taken to gradually abandon the trolleybus network in favour of motorbuses. The fundamental reason for this decision included the inflexibility of trolleybus services which were tied to an overhead system which was not easily adaptable to the increasing number of new road patterns being introduced throughout the city and they had also become expensive, both to run and service. Particularly, the cost of electricity had increased significantly since the end of the 1940s when the city council ceased to run its own electricity undertaking, and the cost of overhead equipment had escalated to a point where the trolleybus was no longer competitive with its motorbus counterpart.

Accordingly, the gradual run-down of the trolleybus system commenced, with the withdrawal of the 13-14 service from Cosham to Southsea on 13th September 1958. This was followed by the 15-16 service and the 19-20 service on 1st May 1960, and in September that year the 3-4 service was replaced by motorbuses and extended to Paulsgrove.

The final death knell of trolleybus operation was sounded by the withdrawal of the 7-8 and 11-12 services at the beginning of December 1961, following which it was intended to replace the two surviving services, the 5-6 and the 17-18, during 1962. However, the replacement vehicles chosen, the Leyland Atlantean 78-seat double deckers, were proving so popular throughout the country that there was over a year's delay in the delivery time for these vehicles, which resulted in a slight reprieve for the two remaining services until the summer of 1963. The 17-18 service finally succumbed on 23rd June 1963, and the 5-6 service on Saturday, 27th July 1963. In fact, the last trolleybuses into the depot were actually on the already replaced 17-18 service which had its final evening journeys run from the Dockyard to Eastney depot by trolleybuses from the 5-6 service, the last bus from which terminated late each evening at the Dockyard, conveniently to provide the last journeys back to Eastney depot on the 17-18 service.

The Portsmouth *News* reported that there were around 150 'mourners' to witness the end of the trolleybus operation, although the end was a low-key affair, there being no official ceremony.

On arrival shortly before midnight the last vehicle was decorated with a large floral wreath placed at the front by Mr A.W.Fielder, the Deputy Manager of the Transport Department and the trolleybus then glided slowly into the depot.

After the closure of the system, most of the surviving trolleybuses were acquired by a scrap metal dealer and towed to a breakers yard at the former city airport. One of the Burlingham's – no. 313 – was acquired for preservation by an enthusiast and has run from time to time at the Sandtoft Trolleybus Museum near Doncaster.

CHRONOLOGY OF TROLLEYBUS ROUTES

4th August 1934	Trolleybus route officially opened: 3-4: Cosham to South Parade Pier via Fratton and Fawcett Roads
3rd November 1935	Trolleybus route 3-4 extended to Cosham via Albert Road, Guildhall, Twyford Avenue and Northern Parade
1st October 1936	New trolleybus route: 1-2: Cosham to Clarence Pier via Guildhall
1st November 1936	New trolleybus routes: 11-12: Copnor Bridge to Dockyard via Lake Road 15-16: Copnor Bridge to Floating Bridge via Lake Road

10th November 1936	Trams Withdrawn - New Trolleybus routes:	
	5-6:	Dockyard to Guildhall via South Parade Pier and Eastney
	17-18:	Dockyard to Dockyard via Eastney and Milton
5th July 1940	WAR CUTS:	
	1-2, 3-4, 5-6 withdrawn from Sea Front area	
17th July 1940	WAR REVISIONS:	
	1-2	diverted to operate via Osborne Road and Victoria Road to North End Junction
	3-4	service revised to operate:
	3-4A	Cosham to The Strand via Fratton Road then to Dockyard over 5-6 route
	3A-4	Cosham to Albert Road via Guildhall then to Guildhall via Milton
	5-6	withdrawn
	15-16	curtailed to operate between Copnor Bridge and Guildhall
	1A-2A	introduced to operate between Cosham and Palmerston Road via Guildhall and extended to Eastney
13th May 1945	5-6	service reinstated between Dockyard and Milton via Southsea
	3-4A	extended to South Parade Pier
1st July 1946	1-2	trolleybus service withdrawn and replaced by new trolleybus routes:
	7-8:	Copnor Bridge to Clarence Pier via Fawcett Road and The Strand
	9-10:	Cosham – Victoria Road – Guildhall - Cosham
	13-14:	Cosham to South Parade Pier via Victoria Road
	3-4A:	Route extended to Alexandra Park via Twyford Avenue
18th May 1947	1-2	trolleybus route withdrawn and replaced by bus service M-N between Farlington-Cosham-Dockyard Trolleybus service 1A-2A renumbered 1-2
26th September 1948	3-4A	service renumbered 3-4
	3A-4	service renumbered 19-20
18th June 1950	Trolley service 1-2 replaced by bus service R-S: Portchester – Southsea - Cosham	
30th September 1951	15-16	Trolley route withdrawn
6th January 1952	7-8 and 11-12 routes extended to Green Lane (Madeira Road terminus) via Copnor Road	
25th May 1952	5-6	service extended to Cosham (Red Lion) via Milton Road and Copnor Road
26th September 1953	9-10	service temporarily suspended – never to be reintroduced

27th September 1953		New trolley service 15-16: Alexandra Park to Eastney via Chichester Road replaced bus service E-F
13th September 1958	13-14	service Cosham to Southsea via Victoria Road withdrawn. Part of this route replaced by Southdown service 45A who increased the frequency within the City
1st May 1960	15-16	service replaced by OMO single deck operation
	19-20	service replaced by double deck operation and route extended to Paulsgrove peak hours and on Saturdays
18th September 1960	3-4	service replaced by double deck operation and route extended to Paulsgrove, Hillsley Road and also replaced service 21: Hillsley Road to Hilsea Lido
3rd December 1961	7-8	service replaced by single deck OMO
	11-12	service replaced by double deck buses and alternative buses operated to and from Ebery Grove (Service 11/12B). Green Lane route numbered 11-12A
23rd June 1963	17-18	service replaced by single deck OMO
27th July 1963	5-6	service replaced by double deck buses

PORTSMOUTH CORPORATION TRAMWAYS

NOTICE!

REORGANISATION OF CAR AND BUS SERVICES
AND
INAUGURATION OF TROLLEY BUSES

With the introduction of a service of Trolley Buses on Saturday the 4th August, 1934, the Services passing through the Fratton and Kingston Roads have been reorganised as under:—

The TROLLEY BUS SERVICE will operate on and after Saturday, 4th August, 1934, directly between Cosham and South Parade Pier and vice-versa, via London Road, Kingston Road, Fratton Road, Fawcett Road, Waverley Road and Clarendon Road, at the following times:—

From COSHAM 6.56 a.m. and every 10 minutes until 10.56 p.m.
" S.P.P. 7.28 a.m. " " " 11. 8 p.m.

SUNDAYS
" COSHAM 9.56 a.m. and every 10 minutes until 10.56 p.m.
" S.P.P. 9.48 a.m. " " " 11. 8 p.m.

The 9 and 10 TRAMCAR SERVICE (Cosham to Palmerston Road and North End) will be discontinued, and substituted by a diversion and extension of the "I" and "J" bus Service (Green Lane and South Parade Pier). Each week-day, in a northerly direction, the "I" and "J" bus route will be extended from the present terminus at Green Lane, via Copnor Road to the Cosham Railway Gates terminus. In a southerly direction the Service passing through Kingston and Fratton Roads will be diverted at Fratton Bridge via Victoria Roads North and South, Clarendon Road, Osborne Road, the Terraces, Guildhall, Commercial Road to North End, and extended to Green Lane via Stubbington Avenue from about mid-day each week-day and as required.

TIMES
From COSHAM 7.49 a.m. and every 10 minutes until 11. 9 p.m.
" GREEN LANE 7.34 a.m. " " " 11.14 p.m.
" NORTH END 7. 0 a.m. " " " 11.30 p.m.

NORTH END to GUILDHALL and PALMERSTON ROAD
From NORTH END 7. 5 a.m. and every 10 minutes until 11.15 p.m.
" GREEN LANE 11.59 a.m. " " " 11. 9 p.m.

On Sundays the "I" and "J" Service will operate only between Cosham and South Parade Pier, via Copnor Road, Stubbington Avenue, Kingston Road, Fratton Road, Victoria Road and Clarendon Road, and vice-versa at the following times:

COSHAM, GREEN LANE and SOUTH PARADE PIER
From COSHAM 9.57½ a.m. and every 7½ minutes until 10.50 p.m.
" GREEN LANE 9.40 a.m. " " " 10.55 p.m.
" NORTH END 9.47 a.m. " " " 11. 2 p.m.

SOUTH PARADE PIER to GREEN LANE and COSHAM
From S.P.P. 9.47½ a.m. and every 7½ minutes until 11.10 p.m.

The 7 and 8 TRAMCAR SERVICE (Copnor and Clarence Pier) will continue to operate at intervals as at present, but between the points Clarence Pier and St. Mary's Road only. Additionally to this and to provide a connection with Copnor, the "K" and "L" Bus Service

G 45—(309) X 3005—Aug. 1934.   Charpentier Ltd. Printers, 40 High St. Portsmouth.

now operated between the Clarence Pier and Fratton Bridge, will be extended from Fratton Bridge, via Fratton Road, New Road, Copnor Bridge, Tangier Road, Neville Road, and terminating at the junction of Hayling Avenue and Kimbolton Road.

TIMES
From HAYLING AVENUE 7.51 a.m. and every 10 minutes until 10.31 p.m.
" CLARENCE PIER 8.22 a.m. " " " 11. 2 p.m.

SUNDAYS
" HAYLING AVENUE 9.51 a.m. and every 10 minutes until 10. 1 p.m.
" CLARENCE PIER 10.2 a.m. " " " 10.32 p.m.

The 3 and 4 TRAMCAR SERVICE (North End to South Parade Pier and Twyford Avenue) will be operated between Twyford Avenue and the Guildhall, and vice-versa, on the following route—Twyford Avenue, Commercial Road, Guildhall, Bradford Junction, Albert Road, Festing Road, South Parade Pier, Clarendon Road, Victoria Road and Bradford Junction, at the following times:—

From TWYFORD AVENUE 7.40 a.m. and every 10 minutes until 11. 1 p.m.
" S. P. PIER 7.51 a.m. " " " 11.21 p.m.
" GUILDHALL 7.38 a.m. " " " 11. 8 p.m.
" S.P.P. to GUILDHALL via Circle
8. 8 a.m. " " " 11.28 p.m.

SUNDAYS
" TWYFORD AVENUE 9.30 a.m. and every 10 minutes until 11. 1 p.m.
" S. P. PIER 10.11 a.m. " " " 11.21 p.m.
" GUILDHALL 9.58 a.m. " " " 11. 8 p.m.
" S.P.P. to GUILDHALL via Circle
9.58 a.m. " " " 11.28 p.m.

FOR FARES—SEE FARE BILLS AS EXHIBITED IN VEHICLES.

WORKMEN'S EARLY MORNING CARS AND BUSES

The Early Morning WORKMEN'S TRAMCAR SERVICE between Cosham and the Dockyard, via Commercial Road, will be operated at 10 minutes instead of 12 minutes intervals.

The TRAMCAR SERVICE between Cosham and Dockyard, via Fratton, will be discontinued, but a Service of Buses will operate between Cosham and Fratton Bridge, commencing from Cosham at 6.0 a.m. and from Fratton Bridge at 6.0 a.m.

The "C" and "D" BUS SERVICE and the LAKE ROAD CAR SERVICES will be augmented to meet the requirements of Dockyard employees residing in Fratton and Buckland districts.

B. HALL, General Manager and Engineer.

1. Introduction of Trolleybus Service

1.   This view taken at Cosham Compound is of no. 14, the first trolleybus to enter service on 4th August 1934. It appears to be a posed photograph showing civic dignitaries as well as some enthusiastic members of the public keen to get in on the act! Next to the trolleybus is no. 7, a Leyland TD1 with Park Royal bodywork, purchased in 1930. In the background can be seen the bridge carrying the Portsdown & Horndean Light Railway over the Portsmouth to Southampton Railway line. (T.Dethridge coll.)

Local tramway albums include
Gosport and Horndean Tramways and
Portsmouth Tramways.

2.　　This splendid view was taken at North End Junction outside the Southdown Offices. No. 14 has just left North End Depot on driver training duties in July 1934. (A.Triggs)

3.　　An interesting line-up at Cosham Compound was also taken on the first day of service and shows trolleybus no. 10 about to depart on its first journey. Also in the picture are Crossley Condor no. 104 with English Electric bodywork and tram no. 70. (G.A.Tucker)

2. Cosham 'Red Lion' to Hilsea

4.   This view was taken at the northernmost point reached by the trolleybus system. No. 248 is turning off the A3 London Road at the foot of Portsdown Hill towards the 'Red Lion' terminus. Queen Alexandra Hospital is in the background behind the embankment which once carried the Portsdown & Horndean Light Railway. (B.R.Cox)

5.   A commercial view of Spur Road taken in 1952 shows one of the new Burlingham bodied BUT trolleybus no. 305 on route 10 which was suspended later that year, at the 'Red Lion' terminus. Note the overhead passing loop. Although never used, there were powers to extend the trolleybus system to Farlington along Havant Road which is the road in the background beyond the traffic lights. (Postcard)

6.   A Burlingham is seen here in the early summer of 1963 outside Cosham Police Station. The Police Station was built in the mid-1950s for the former Portsmouth City Police Force which was absorbed into the Hampshire Force upon local government reorganisation in 1974. (B.R.Cox)

7. A somewhat neglected-looking no. 220 from the 1935 batch of AEC trolleybuses with English Electric bodywork stands at Cosham Compound which was accessed from 1942 along the Private Road seen in the background. A Craven-bodied Leyland TD4 can also be seen travelling north towards Northern Road Bridge. Note the ornate shelter which still remains. (T.Dethridge coll.)

8.   This view of no. 311 was also taken at Cosham Compound – the terminus for Cosham Railway station. In the background can be seen Cosham railway gates themselves. (V.C.Jones)

9.   This view was taken at the same spot as the photo above, but shows clearly how the 19-20 service used the outer line of wires whilst services 3-4 and 13-14 were allocated the inner line. (L.Bushill coll.)

10.   No. 31 is seen here on a 'Special' to South Parade Pier in 1937 just south of Highbury Buildings, heading towards Portsbridge. Chatsworth Avenue is off to the right in the background. Note the white roof. (G.A.Tucker)

Corporation Trolley Bus Service 3	COSHAM (Railway Gates) — SOUTHSEA (South Parade Pier) Via London Road, North End Junction, Kingston Road, Fratton Road, Fawcett Road, Waverley Road and Strand.	Corporation Trolley Bus Service 3

WEEKDAY SERVICE

Cosham *Railway Gates* ...	6‡57	7‡ 9	7‡21	7 33	7 45	7 57	8 9	8 21	8 33	8 45	8 57	9 9	9 21	9 33	9 45	9 57	10 9	1021	1033
North End *Junction* ...	7 6	7 18	7 30	7 42	7 54	8 6	8 18	8 30	8 42	8 54	9 6	9 18	9 30	9 42	9 54	10 6	1018	1030	1042
Fratton Bridge ...	7 15	7 27	7 39	7 51	8 3	8 15	8 27	8 39	8 51	9 3	9 15	9 27	9 39	9 51	10 3	1015	1027	1039	1051
Southsea *South Parade Pier* ...	7 23	7 35	7 47	7 59	8 11	8 23	8 35	8 47	8 59	9 11	9 23	9 35	9 47	9 59	1011	1023	1035	1047	1059

Cosham *Railway Gates* ...	1045	1057	and at the	9	21	33	45	57	until	10 9	1021	1033	1045	1057	11 9	1116	1128	
North End *Junction* ...	1054	11 6	following	18	30	42	54	6		1018	1030	1042	1054	11 6	1118	1125	1137	
Fratton Bridge ...	11 3	1115	minutes past	27	39	51	3	15		1027	1039	1051	11 3	1115	1127	...	...	
Southsea *South Parade Pier* ...	1111	1123	each hour	35	47	59	11	23		1035	1047	1059	1111					

SUNDAY SERVICE

Cosham *Railway Gates* ...	8 15	8 45	9 15	9 30	9 45	10 0	1015	1030	1045	11 0	1115	1130	1145	12 0	1215	1230	1245	1257	1 9	1 21
North End *Junction* ...	8 24	8 54	9 24	9 39	9 54	10 9	1024	1039	1054	11 9	1124	1139	1154	12 9	1224	1239	1254	1 6	1 18	1 30
Fratton Bridge ...	8 33	9 3	9 33	9 48	10 3	1018	1033	1048	11 3	1118	1133	1148	12 3	1218	1233	1248	1 3	1 15	1 27	1 39
Southsea *South Parade Pier* ...	8 41	9 11	9 41	9 56	1011	1026	1041	1056	1111	1126	1141	1156	1211	1226	1241	1256	1 11	1 23	1 35	1 47

Cosham *Railway Gates* ...	1 33	1 45	1 57	and at the	9	21	33	45	57	until	10 9	1021	1033	1045	1057	11 9	1116	1128
North End *Junction* ...	1 42	1 54	2 6	following	18	30	42	54	6		1018	1030	1042	1054	11 6	1118	1125	1137
Fratton Bridge ...	1 51	2 3	2 15	mins. past	27	39	51	3	15		1027	1039	1051	11 3	1115	1127	...	...
Southsea *South Parade Pier* ...	1 59	2 11	2 23	each hour	35	47	59	11	23		1035	1047	1059	1111				

11.   A panoramic view of Portsbridge set against the backdrop of Fort Widley on the summit of Portsdown Hill, shows no. 21 heading south on route 3 bound for South Parade Pier. The trolleybus in the background is turning right bound for the Cosham Railway station terminus. The motorbus in the view is no. 84. By this time the tramlines which ran in the centre of the bridge have been removed or covered over. (T.Dethridge coll.)

12.   A bustling scene taken about 1953 is outside the Southdown Garage at Hilsea. There are no fewer than seven buses or coaches and two trolleybuses in this view! In the foreground no. 275 is en route to North End on a short working from Cosham. The trolleybus coming off Portsbridge is on route 13 to South Parade Pier. Amongst others in the view are two Southdown Utility Guy Arabs, a Portsmouth Corporation Bedford OWB and a pre-war Southdown Leyland Tigar coach. (B.R.Cox coll.)

3. Hilsea to Pier Hotel via Commercial Road and Guildhall

13.   Our first view is about a mile south of Hilsea at Alexandra Park terminus in the late 1950s. In the foreground is an AEC Craven-bodied trolleybus on route 19-20. In the background a Burlingham-bodied BUT is about to depart for Eastney on route 16. (G.A.Tucker)

14.   Travelling south we reach Mile End and this shot taken in 1957 shows no. 232 on route 20 passing the ornate colonnade of the Mile End Cemetery which was demolished in 1958. The Ferry Port now covers part of the cemetery. (G.A.Tucker)

15.   During World War II Portsmouth suffered badly from a number of intensive bombing raids which seriously affected the trolleybus services, particularly in the city centre. This view, taken in April 1941, shows Commercial Road roughly at the spot where Market Way is today. Pedestrians pick their way through the rubble while workmen on TW1, one of the two pre-war Dennis tower wagons, are seen rehanging the overhead wires.
(Courtesy of the *News*, Portsmouth)

16.   The last day of trolleybus operation on the 11-12 service was a wet Saturday in early December 1961. Here, no 233 is seen at the junction of Lake Road with Commercial Road en route to the Dockyard. The tarpaulins on the right are protecting passers-by from the demolition work in progress on the former landmark 'Emperor of India' public house. (B.R.Cox)

17.   A bustling scene of Commercial Road near Edinburgh Road (on left) in 1937 includes no. 90 is on a special working to Cosham 'Red Lion' whilst the vehicle in front is on Service 2 to Cosham 'Red Lion'. Also to be seen, near the platform of no. 90, is a white plate bearing the number 890 – this was a Hackney Carriage registration plate also carried by public service vehicles in Portsmouth at this time. (T.Dethridge coll.)

18. It is possible to count 13 buses and trolleybuses in this evocative view of early post-war Commercial Road, taken from the high level at Portsmouth & Southsea station. No. 271 on route 1A is the only identifiable trolleybus and the Bedford OWB in the foreground bears the insignia of the Royal Navy Transport Department. (T.Dethridge coll.)

19.   There seems to be some distraction here, judging by the direction of the gaze of most of the passers-by! No. 21 is heading for Cosham Railway station, whilst tram no. 105 of 1920 vintage is heading in the opposite direction for the Dockyard. This 1936 view showing the old GPO Building on the left is taken from under Portsmouth & Southsea high level station in Commercial Road. It clearly shows how both sets of tramlines ran on the same side of the road at this point. Horsedrawn traffic is also much in evidence. (T.Dethridge coll.)

No. 1—" Red Lion " Hotel, Cosham to Clarence Pier ....
No. 2—Clarence Pier to " Red Lion " Hotel, Cosham ....
No. 3—Cosham to South Parade Pier via Fratton Bridge ....
No. 3—South Parade Pier to Cosham via Festing Road, Albert Road, Guildhall and
      Twyford Avenue ....
No. 4—Cosham to South Parade Pier via Twyford Avenue, Guildhall, Albert Road
      and Festing Road ....
No. 4—South Parade Pier to Cosham via Fratton Bridge ....
No. 5—Dockyard to South Parade Pier via Palmerston Road, then to Eastney, Milton
      and Guildhall ....
No. 6—Guildhall, Milton, Eastney to South Parade Pier and Dockyard (via Palmerston
      Road) ....
No. 11—Copnor to Dockyard via Guildhall ....
No. 12—Dockyard to Copnor via Guildhall ....
No. 15—Copnor to Floating Bridge via Guildhall ....
No. 16—Floating Bridge to Copnor via Guildhall ....
No. 17—Dockyard to Eastney via Albert Road, then to Milton, Guildhall and Dockyard
No. 18—Dockyard to Eastney via Milton, then via Albert Road, Guildhall and Dockyard

1939

1958

LIST OF PORTSMOUTH AREA JOINT TRANSPORT SERVICES

City of Portsmouth Passenger Transport Dept.

TROLLEY BUS SERVICES

20.   This scene recorded in the late 1950s, clearly shows the complex wiring at the busy junction of Greetham Street and the Guildhall Square. It was still safe for policemen to stand in the middle of the road directing traffic in those days! Portsmouth & Southsea station can be seen in the background. (T.Dethridge coll.)

21.   No. 265 is seen here still in ornate livery in the late 1940s on an enthusiast's tour of the system. This shot is unique because it shows a trolleybus travelling from Park Road south into Commercial Road. As there was no overhead wiring to perform this manoeuvre, the vehicle is travelling the short distance on its batteries. (T.Dethridge coll.)

22.   Immediately south of the Guildhall Square was the continuation of Commercial Road, now Guildhall Walk. No. 224 is seen here in the mid-1950s at the stop outside the bomb site of the Hippodrome Theatre. (T.Dethridge coll.)

23.   Travelling south along 'The Terraces' one reaches Kings Terrace, and no. 251 is seen here on the old route 5 en route to 'White House' Milton in 1951, next to yet another bomb site. The building which stands on the corner of Kings Road once housed the Abbey National Building Society. (B.R.Cox coll.)

24.   The last of 'The Terraces' is Bellevue Terrace, at the end of which is situated the Pier Hotel – now rebuilt and converted to a hall of residence for Portsmouth University students. No. 267 can be seen in 1952 en route to Cosham 'Red Lion' via Palmerston Road. (B.R.Cox coll.)

4. Hilsea to The Strand via North End and Fratton Bridge

25.   This close-up view of no. 2 was taken in 1935 outside the 'Coach and Horses' at Hilsea. In the background coming out of Copnor Road can be seen a Karrier 6-wheeler with either Brush or English Electric bodywork. (G.A.Tucker)

26.   This view, taken outside Gatcombe Barracks at Hilsea in August 1934 shortly after the trolleybus operation began, shows clearly the separation of the wiring between the trolleybuses and the trams still running along this section at the time. (T.Dethridge coll.)

27.   We can examine the wiring layout coming out of Gladys Avenue, North End, into London Road. Seen here again is the somewhat neglected looking no. 220 about to head for Cosham. No. 218 is about to run into the Depot after completing a short working on route 14. (T.Dethridge coll.)

28.   This 1936 view of no. 22, an AEC with English Electric bodywork, was taken at North End Junction looking towards the Southdown office on the corner of Gladys Avenue. Noteworthy in the view is Percy Tuck's Newsagency and Tobacconists, which was well patronised by both crews and passengers using the stop outside. (T.Dethridge coll.)

29.   A 1935 view features no. 15 at North End outside the 'Clarence' public house. The premises next door are run by White & Co. Limited, a well-known Portsmouth firm of furnishers and removers. Also Melanies, the noted Co-op Departmental Store at North End, can just be seen on the left. (G.A.Tucker)

Corporation Trolley Bus Service 13	COSHAM (Railway Gates) — SOUTHSEA (South Parade Pier) Via London Road, North End Junction, Fratton Road, Victoria Road, Circle and Strand.	Corporation Trolley Bus Service 13

WEEKDAYS ONLY (No Service on Sundays)

Cosham *Railway Gates* ...	8‡ 3 8 15 8 27 8 39 8 51 9 3 9 15 9 27 9 39 9 51 10 3 1015 1027 1039 1051 11 3 1115 1127 1139 1151 12 3
North End *Junction* ...	8 12 8 24 8 36 8 48 9 0 9 12 9 24 9 36 9 48 10 0 1012 1024 1036 1048 11 0 1112 1124 1136 1148 12 0 1212
Fratton Bridge ...	8 21 8 33 8 45 8 57 9 9 9 21 9 33 9 45 9 57 10 9 1021 1033 1045 1057 11 9 1121 1133 1145 1157 12 9 1221
Southsea *South Parade Pier*	8 29 8 41 8 53 9 5 9 17 9 29 9 41 9 53 10 5 1017 1029 1041 1053 11 5 1117 1129 1141 1153 12 5 1217 1229

Cosham *Railway Gates* ...	1215 1227 1239 1251 1 3 1 15 1 27 1 39 1 51 2 3 2 15 2 27 2 39 2 51 3 3 3 15 3 27 3 39 3 51 4 3 4 15
North End *Junction* ...	1224 1236 1248 1 0 1 12 1 24 1 36 1 48 2 0 2 12 2 24 2 36 2 48 3 0 3 12 3 24 3 36 3 48 4 0 4 12 4 24
Fratton Bridge ...	1233 1245 1257 1 9 1 21 1 33 1 45 1 57 2 9 2 21 2 33 2 45 2 57 3 9 3 21 3 33 3 45 3 57 4 9 4 21 4 33
Southsea *South Parade Pier*	1241 1253 1 5 1 17 1 29 1 41 1 53 2 5 2 17 2 29 2 41 2 53 3 5 3 17 3 29 3 41 3 53 4 5 4 17 4 29 4 41

Cosham *Railway Gates* ...	4 27 4 39 4 51 5 3 5 15 5 27 5 39 5 51 6 3 6 15 6 27 6 39 6 51 7 3 7 15 7 27 7 39 7 51 8 3 ... ...
North End *Junction* ...	4 36 4 48 5 0 5 12 5 24 5 36 5 48 6 0 6 12 6 24 6 36 6 48 7 0 7 12 7 24 7 36 7 48 8 0 8 12 ... ...
Fratton Bridge ...	4 45 4 57 5 9 5 21 5 33 5 45 5 57 6 9 6 21 6 33 6 45 6 57 7 9 7 21 7 33 7 45 7 57 8 9 8 21 ... ...
Southsea *South Parade Pier*	4 53 5 5 5 17 5 29 5 41 5 53 6 5 6 17 6 29 6 41 6 53 7 5 7 17 7 29 7 41 7 53 8 5 8 17 8 29 ... ...

30.   This late-1940s view shows no. 218, one of the 1935 batch of AECs with English Electric bodywork, en route to South Parade Pier on route 3. (T.Dethridge coll.)

31.   A scene of wartime destruction in 1941 at Kingston Cross includes No. 273, showing destination screen blank, heading towards North End on route 4A to Cosham. Note the armed guard – there to deter looters. (B.R.Cox coll.)

32.   An early view – perhaps 1935 – of no. 24 outside St Mary's Church shows it on a special working to South Parade Pier. (B.R.Cox coll.)

33. Further down Fratton Road, approaching Fratton Bridge, no. 253 is seen outside the former Wesley Central Hall in October 1961 shortly before routes 7-8 were converted to motorbuses. (B.R.Cox)

34. All the buildings in this mid-1950s scene near Fratton Bridge have long since been demolished. No. 201 is on a short working on route 4 to North End. (T.Dethridge coll.)

35.   A study in overhead wiring! The Portsmouth system was notable for a number of complex overhead layouts and this example at Fratton Bridge taken in 1937 is a superb example. The building in the background was the Fratton Hotel which was destroyed in World War II. Note the semaphore signal. (T.Dethridge coll.)

36.   Continuing over Fratton Bridge and into Fawcett Road, one reaches Rugby Road. This was unique in being fully wired although no services were actually scheduled to run along it. (B.R.Cox)

37.   This view clearly shows the right-angled overhead crossing at Albert Road and Waverley Road. The driver is heading north on route 8 in 1961. (B.R.Cox)

38.   Continuing along Waverley Road we reach The Strand at its junction with Clarendon Road about half a mile from South Parade Pier on what looks like a fine summer's day in the mid-1950s. (T.Dethridge coll.)

5. Hilsea to South Parade Pier via Copnor Road

39.   Our journey along Copnor Road commences about a mile south of Hilsea at the Green Lane terminus of routes 7-8 and 11-12. Although the destination was known as Green Lane, in fact the terminus itself was on the opposite side of the road in Madeira Road. No. 252 is seen pulling out of Madeira Road into Copnor Road en route to the Dockyard on a fine autumn day in 1961. (B.R.Cox)

40.   Turning at the Madeira Road terminus was effected by way of a 'three-point turn'. No.244 is at the limit of the wiring in Madeira Road and is about to reverse into Compton Road on the right. It will then pull out back into Madeira Road facing towards Copnor Road which can be seen in the background where a Leyland PD2 with MCW Orion bodywork can be seen passing. (B.R.Cox)

41.   Continuing along Copnor Road, this view is taken at the junction with Chichester Road which formed a part of the last trolleybus route to be opened in Portsmouth – the 15-16 from Eastney to Alexandra Park in 1953. A Burlingham on route 5 traverses the junction in the autumn of 1961. Note the police telephone pillar on the corner. (B.R.Cox)

42.   No. 307 is seen here pulling in at Copnor Bridge. The bus shelter in the view is noteworthy. (B.R.Cox)

Corporation Trolley Bus Service 6	COSHAM (Red Lion) — COPNOR — MILTON — EASTNEY — SOUTH PARADE PIER — DOCKYARD	Corporation Trolley Bus Service 6

Via Northern Road, Cosham Railway Station, Portsmouth Road, London Road, Copnor Road, Milton Road, Eastney Road, Highland Road, Festing Road, South Parade Pier, Strand, Osborne Road, Western Parade, King's Road Junction and Cambridge Junction.

SUNDAY SERVICE

Cosham *Red Lion*	…	…	…	…	…	…	…	1016	1031	1046	11 1	1116	1131	1146	12 1	1216	1231	1246	1 1	16	1 31		
Cosham *Railway Gates*	…	…	…	…	…	…	…	1019	1034	1049	11 4	1119	1134	1149	12 4	1219	1234	1249	1 4	19	1 34		
Copnor Bridge	…	…	…	…	…	…	1031	1046	11 1	1116	1131	1146	12 1	1216	1231	1246	1 1	16	1 31	46			
Milton *White House*	…	…	9 21	9 36	9 51	10 6	1021	1036	1051	11 6	1121	1136	1151	12 6	1221	1236	1251	1 6	21	1 36	1 51	
Eastney	…	…	9 23	9 38	9 53	10 8	1023	1038	1053	11 8	1123	1138	1153	12 8	1223	1238	1253	1 8	23	1 38	1 53	
Southsea *South Parade Pier*	…	…	9 29	9 44	9 59	1014	1029	1044	1059	1114	1129	1144	1159	1214	1229	1244	1259	1 14	29	1 44	1 59	
Palmerston Road	…	…	9 33	9 48	10 3	1018	1033	1048	11 3	1118	1133	1148	12 3	1218	1233	1248	1 3	18	1 33	48	2 3	
Dockyard *Main Gate*	…	…	9 42	9 57	1012	1027	1042	1057	1112	1127	1142	1157	1212	1227	1242	1257	1 12	27	1 42	1 57	2 12	

Cosham *Red Lion*	…	1 46		1	16	31	46		9 1	9 16	9 32	9 48	10 4	1020	1034	10 46	11 4	1116	
Cosham *Railway Gates*	…	1 49		4	19	34	49		9 4	9 19	9 35	9 51	10 7	1023	1037	10 49	11 7	1119	
Copnor Bridge	…	2 1	and at the	16	31	46	1		9 16	9 31	9 47	10 3	1019	1035	1049	11 1	1119	1131	
Milton *White House*	…	2 6	following	21	36	51	6	until	9 21	9 36	9 52	10 8	1024	1040	1054	11 6	1124	1136	
Eastney	…	2 8	minutes	23	38	53	8		9 23	9 38	9 54	1010	1026	1042	1056	11 8	1126	1138	
Southsea *South Parade Pier*	…	2 14	past each	29	44	59	14		9 29	9 44	10 0	1016	1032	1048	11 2	11 14	…	…	
Palmerston Road	…	2 18	hour	33	48	3	18		9 33	9 48	10 4	1020	1036	1052	11 6	11 18	…	…	
Dockyard *Main Gate*	…	2 27		42	57	12	27		9 42	9 57	1013	1029	1045	11 1	1115		…	…	

43.	Snow in Portsmouth is a rare occurrence. In this view an unidentifiable Craven-bodied AEC is seen at Copnor Bridge on a winter's day in 1962. (B.R.Cox)

44.	This view, taken in 1961, shows no. 273 en route to Clarence Pier, waiting to turn into New Road at Copnor Bridge. Copnor Road stretches into the distance with the tower at Copnor Fire Station just visible, and the 'Swan' public House and St Alban's Church in the distance. (B.R.Cox)

45.   No. 259 is seen here on the turning circle at the Copnor Bridge end of New Road. This was used for short workings of the 7-8 and 11-12 routes. (B.R.Cox)

Corporation Trolley Bus Service 11	GREEN LANE—COPNOR BRIDGE—GUILDHALL—DOCKYARD Via Copnor Road, New Road, Lake Road, Commercial Road, Guildhall and Park Road.	Corporation Trolley Bus Service 11

MONDAY TO FRIDAY SERVICE

```
Green Lane        ...   ...    ...   ...   ...   ...    6 21  ...   ...   6 31  ...   6 41  ...   6 53  ...   7  5  ...   7 20  ...   7 35
Copnor Bridge     ...   5 30  5 45  6  0  6 10  6 15  6 20  6 25  6 30  6 33  6 35  6 40  6 45  6 51  6 57  7  3  7  9  7 16  7 24  7 31  7 39  7 46
Guildhall         ...   5 41  5 56  6 11  6 21  6 26  6 31  6 36  6 41  6 44  6 46  6 51  6 56  7  2  7  8  7 14  7 20  7 27  7 35  7 42  7 50  7 57
Dockyard Main Gate ...  5 45  6  0  6 15  6 25  6 30  6 35  6 40  6 45  6 48  6 50  6 55  7  0  7  6  7 12  7 18  7 24  7 31  7 39  7 46  7 54  8

Green Lane        ...   7 50  ...   8  5  ...   8 20  ...   8 35  ...   8 50  ...   9  5  ...   9 20  ...   9 35  ...   9 50  ...   10 5  ...   1020
Copnor Bridge     ...   7 54  8  1  8  9  8 16  8 24  8 31  8 39  8 46  8 54  9  1  9  9  9 16  9 24  9 31  9 39  9 46  9 54  10 1  10 9  1016  1024
Guildhall         ...   8  5  8 12  8 20  8 27  8 35  8 42  8 50  8 57  9  5  9 12  9 20  9 27  9 35  9 42  9 50  9 57  10 5  1012  1020  1027  1035
Dockyard Main Gate ...  8  9  8 16  8 24  8 31  8 39  8 46  8 54  9  1  9  9  9 16  9 24  9 31  9 39  9 46  9 54  10 1  10 9  1016  1024  1031  1039

Green Lane        ...   ...   1035  ...   1050           and at          ...   5  ...  20  ...  35  ...  50         until   ...   4  5  ...   4 17  ...   4 29
Copnor Bridge     ...   1031  1039  1046  1054       the following        1   9  16  24  31  39  46  54                 4  4  4  9  4 15  4 21  4 27  4 33  4 39
Guildhall         ...   1042  1050  1057  11 5        minutes past       12  20  27  35  42  50  57   5                 4 12  4 20  4 26  4 32  4 38  4 44  4 50
Dockyard Main Gate ...  1046  1054  11 1  11 9          each hour        16  24  31  39  46  54   1   9                 4 16  4 24  4 30  4 36  4 42  4 48  4 54

Green Lane        ...   4 41  ...   4 53  ...   5  5  ...   5 17  ...   5 29  ...   5 41  ...   5 53  ...   6  5  ...   6 24  ...   6 44
Copnor Bridge     ...   4 45  4 51  4 57  5  3  5  9  5 15  5 21  5 27  5 33  5 39  5 45  5 51  5 57  6  3  6  9  6 18  6 28  6 38  6 48
Guildhall         ...   4 56  5  2  5  8  5 14  5 20  5 26  5 32  5 38  5 44  5 50  5 56  6  2  6  8  6 14  6 20  6 29  6 39  6 49  6 59
Dockyard Main Gate ...  5  0  5  6  5 12  5 18  5 24  5 30  5 36  5 42  5 48  5 54  6  0  6  6  6 12  6 18  6 24  6 33  6 43  6 53  7  3

Green Lane        ...   ...   6 58        then at          4  ...  24  ...  44  ...        10 4  ...  1024  ...  1044  ...  11 5  1125  ...   ...
Copnor Bridge     ...   6 58          the following        8  18  28  38  48  58          10 8  1018  1028  1038  1048  1058  11 9  ...   ...
Guildhall         ...   7  9          minutes past        19  29  39  49  59   9   until  1019  1029  1039  1049  1059  11 9  1120   To North End
Dockyard Main Gate ...  7 13            each hour          23  33  43  53   3  13          1023  1033  1043  1053  11 3  1113  1124   via Copnor Rd.
                                                                                                                               & Chichester Rd
```

46.   No. 311 lists to port in this view taken in 1961 at the junction of Milton Road and St Mary's Road. (B.R.Cox)

47.   No. 307 is seen at Milton White House at the junction of Milton Road and Goldsmith Avenue. The garage forecourt opposite is on the line of the old Arundel-Portsmouth Canal. The railway from Fratton to Portsmouth & Southsea Station was constructed in 1847 in the cutting along the line used by the canal. (B.R.Cox)

48. Travelling south from the 'White House', one comes to Bransbury Park and this scene shows no. 308 passing the Essoldo cinema on the corner of Devonshire Avenue. The cinema has been demolished since this 1961 view was taken. (B.R.Cox)

Corporation Trolley Bus Service 5		DOCKYARD — SOUTH PARADE PIER — EASTNEY — MILTON — COPNOR — COSHAM (Red Lion)									Corporation Trolley Bus Service 5

Via Cambridge Junction, King's Road Junction, Western Parade, Osborne Road, Strand, South Parade Pier, Festing Road, Highland Road, Eastney Road, Milton Road, Copnor Road, London Road and Northern Road.

WEEKDAY SERVICE

Dockyard *Main Gate*	...	...	...	6 47	6 59	7 11	7 23	7 35	7 47	7 59	8 11	8 23	8 35	8 47	8 59	9 11	9 23	9 35	9 47	9 59	1011
Palmerston Road	...	...	...	6 56	7 8	7 20	7 32	7 44	7 56	8 8	8 20	8 32	8 44	8 56	9 8	9 20	9 32	9 44	9 56	10 8	1020
Southsea *South Parade Pier*	...	...	...	7 0	7 12	7 24	7 36	7 48	8 0	8 12	8 24	8 36	8 48	9 0	9 12	9 24	9 36	9 48	10 0	1012	1024
Eastney	...	...	...	...	...	...	...	7 54	8 6	8 18	8 30	8 42	8 54	9 6	9 18	9 30	9 42	9 54	10 6	1018	1030
Milton *White House*	...	...	...	...	...	...	...	7 56	8 8	8 20	8 32	8 44	8 56	9 8	9 20	9 32	9 44	9 56	10 8	1020	1032
Copnor Bridge	...	...	...	...	...	...	...	8 1	8 13	8 25	8 37	8 49	9 1	9 13	9 25	9 37	9 49	10 1	1013	1025	1037
Cosham *Railway Bridge*	...	...	...	...	...	...	...	8 13	8 25	8 37	8 49	9 1	9 13	9 25	9 37	9 49	10 1	1013	1025	1037	1049
Cosham *Red Lion*	...	...	...	...	...	...	...	8 16	8 28	8 40	8 52	9 4	9 16	9 28	9 40	9 52	10 4	1016	1028	1040	1052

Dockyard *Main Gate*	...	...	...	1023	1035	1047	1059		11	23	35	47	59		1011	1023	1035	1047	1059	1111
Palmerston Road	...	...	...	1032	1044	1056	11 8	and at	20	32	44	56	8		1020	1032	1044	1056	11 8	1120
Southsea *South Parade Pier*	...	...	...	1036	1048	11 0	1112	the	24	36	48	0	12		1024	1036	1048	11 0	1112	1124
Eastney	...	...	...	1042	1054	11 6	1118	following	30	42	54	6	18	until	1030	1042	1054	11 6	1118	1130
Milton *White House*	...	...	...	1044	1056	11 8	1120	minutes	32	44	56	8	20		1032	1044	1056	11 8	1120	1132
Copnor Bridge	...	...	...	1049	11 1	1113	1125	past each	37	49	1	13	25		1037	1049	11 1	...	...	...
Cosham *Railway Bridge*	...	...	...	11 1	1113	1125	1137	hour	49	1	13	25	37		1049	11 1	1113	...	...	...
Cosham *Red Lion*	...	...	...	11 4	1116	1128	1140		52	4	16	28	40		1052	11 4	1116	...	...	...

49.   A very smart-looking no. 301 is seen opposite Eastney Depot en route to Palmerston Road via South Parade Pier. (B.R.Cox coll.)

50.   We stand near the entrance to Eastney Depot in 1963. The Leyland Leopard with Weymann bodywork no. 143 on the right formed part of a batch purchased in 1963 and is seen here on the 15-16 service to Alexandra Park which, until 1960, had been operated by trolleybuses. Highland Road runs off to the right behind no. 143. The current supply cables are evident. (B.R.Cox)

51.   At the end of Highland Road the 5-6 service turned left in Festing Road towards the seafront. No. 312 is seen here in 1962 opposite the 'Festing Hotel'. (B.R.Cox)

52.   In this 1950s view, no. 302 is seen passing Canoe Lake approaching the South Parade Pier stop for this service. (B.R.Cox coll)

6. Dockyard to Eastney via Milton

53.   This view, taken opposite St George's Square, shows Burlingham no. 304. In the background can be seen the Dockyard terminus and the large boathouses just inside the Main Gate. (B.R.Cox coll.)

54.   In this 1962 view, no. 300 can be seen on route 17 bound for Eastney entering Park Road, having passed under the railway bridge leading to Portsmouth Harbour station. Immediately adjacent to the bridge is the entrance to the new Gunwharf Quays shopping, leisure, housing and entertainment complex built on the site of the former HMS Vernon naval establishment. (B.R.Cox)

55.   This view is of the Guildhall end of Park Road just showing the old swimming baths and the rear of the former Central Library building. On the left is the elevated section of the railway between Portsmouth & Southsea and Portsmouth Harbour stations. When this was taken in 1961, the advertisement for Pompey shows that their forthcoming games were against Brentford, Cardiff and Brighton. (B.R.Cox)

56.   A 1961 view again, taken in the opposite direction from the previous one, showing one of the Burlinghams heading for Milton and Eastney and including the stand for the United Services Rugby and Cricket ground at Burnaby Road on the left. Also in the picture on the right is the elevated section of the railway between the two stations. (B.R.Cox)

57.   Craven no. 300 is seen at the end of Park Road at the stop next to the Guildhall on a gloomy day in 1962. The building in the background is the former Central Library which now forms part of the University of Portsmouth. (B.R.Cox)

59.   A Burlingham was recorded against the background of the imposing Guildhall in April 1963. (B.R.Cox)

58.   No. 274 can be seen here in December 1961 passing the old Corporation Stables en route to the Dockyard. The somewhat imposing building on the left was formerly the Gas Company's offices but is now a Weatherspoons public house. (B.R.Cox)

60.   In this view, also taken in the Spring of 1963, no. 302 is at the end of Greetham Street outside the Sussex Hotel and is about to cross the Guildhall Square into Park Road. (B.R.Cox)

61.   No. 299 is crossing the Guildhall Square on a sunny day in 1963. (B.R.Cox coll.)

62.   In this early 1963 view, no. 246 is pictured in Greetham Street against the backdrop of the Guildhall. The Sussex Hotel is on the left, with a Southdown 'Queen Mary' visible crossing the Guildhall Square. (B.R.Cox)

63.   This view is taken further along the cobbled Greetham Street adjacent to the railway sidings and includes a trolleybus heading for Eastney on route 17. (B.R.Cox)

64.   There was a saying that Portsmouth had a pub on each street corner. In this picture, taken from 'Jacobs Ladder', the 'Morning Star' can be seen on the left and the 'Blackfriars Tavern' on the right. In this April 1963 view, no. 310 is just ahead of a smart looking Crossley recently repainted with white roof on converted trolleybus route no. 20 heading for Cosham Railway station. This sharp corner was also the scene of one of only two major trolleybus accidents during the history of the system, when a trolleybus collided with the front of the 'Morning Star'. (B.R.Cox)

65.   No. 302 is seen here in this 1963 view of a run-down looking Blackfriars Road which has now almost all been redeveloped. (B.R.Cox)

66.   We are at the junction of Blackfriars Road, Somers Road and Bradford Road in 1962. The jewellers and pawnbrokers in the view has long since been demolished. (B.R.Cox)

67.   In this view taken opposite the Gaumont no. 289 is en route to Eastney via Fratton Bridge and Milton. (A. Lambert)

68.   Bradford Road, seen in the previous view, ran into Bradford Junction, and no. 315 can be seen at the stop outside of the Gaumont which was showing '55 Days at Peking'. In the background can be seen the unusual triangular shelter which originated in the days of the trams. In the left background can be seen the entrance to Rugby Road which ran through into Fawcett Road. Victoria Road North runs off to the right behind the trolleybus. (B.R.Cox)

69.	In this delightful 1935 view, no. 7 is seen on the original route 4 at Bradford Junction just about to enter into Victoria Road North en route to South Parade Pier. Note that only the tramwires are in situ on the right-hand side of this view – the trolleybus wires were not erected until November 1935. (T.Dethridge coll.)

70.	This view, taken on the south side of Fratton Bridge, shows no. 248 traversing the complex overhead at this point. The bank and houses in the background have been demolished to make way for road improvements. (B.R.Cox)

71.	Travelling westwards from Fratton Bridge along Goldsmith Avenue we reach Fratton Park, the home of Portsmouth Football Club. In this view, it is clear that Pompey are at home and what appears to be a large crowd is hurrying on its way towards the Frogmore Road entrance to the ground. The three trolleybuses in this 1937 view are all Craven-bodied AECs with no. 30 at the rear. The first vehicle is on the original no. 6 route from the Dockyard. (T.Dethridge coll.)

72.   Goldsmith Avenue formed the junction with Milton Road at the White House where there was another complex set of overhead wires. In this view, no. 248 is seen waiting to come out into Milton Road, and in the background can be seen a Corporation Bedford OWB waiting at the stop opposite Locksway Road at the terminus of the short special hospital service which ran down Locksway Road to St James' Hospital. (B.R.Cox)

73.   No. 302 is seen in 1963 passing 'The Cumberland Tavern' public house which stood on the corner of Eastney Road and Bransbury Road opposite Devonshire Avenue. This has now been converted into flats. (B.R.Cox)

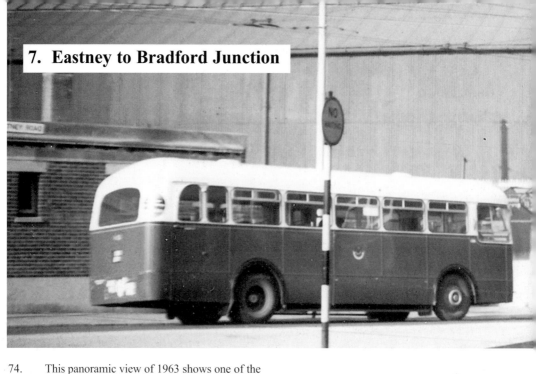

74.   This panoramic view of 1963 shows one of the
Burlinghams passing Eastney Depot on route 6 heading
for South Parade Pier and the Dockyard. It is about to
pass a Leyland Leopard with Weymann bodywork at
the terminus of the 15-16 service from Alexandra Park.
(B.R.Cox)

75.   The beginning of Highland Road was the
handover point for crews on the routes travelling south
past Eastney Depot and in this 1963 view no. 294 is
seen passing no. 308 waiting for its crew. This picture
clearly demonstrates one of the obvious problems of
trolleybuses, namely that one could not pass the other
in the same line without the poles being stowed. In the
background can be seen the 'Eastney Cellars' public
house which stood on the corner of Henderson Road at
that time. (B.R.Cox)

76.   This view, taken further along Highland Road near Prince Albert Road shows no. 314 heading towards Eastney. The destination screen has already been changed to show the Dockyard on this Circular route. (B.R.Cox)

←———

77.   This 1936 photo features no. 5, a Leyland with English Electric bodywork at the Festing, on the no. 3 service via Twyford Avenue, which was opened in November 1935. This is approximately the spot where the old East Southsea Branch railway line which closed in 1914 crossed under a bridge on its way to its destination in Granada Road. (T.Dethridge coll.)

78.   This interesting view, taken further along Albert Road, shows no. 308 at the Kings Theatre. The Kings Theatre, a most noteworthy building, has undergone an uncertain future over the past few years but recently has been saved by the intervention of the city council. In this 1963 view the former 'Essoldo' cinema in Albert Road can also be seen. (B.R.Cox)

79.   This 1963 photograph was taken at the junction of Albert Road with Victoria Road South at the Elm Grove junction. In the background can be seen Victoria Road South, complete with tramlines and granite setts. Albert Road Police Station – now a public house, can be seen on the extreme left of this view. (B.R.Cox)

80.   This view taken in 1962 shows clearly the unique 3-sided shelter at Bradford Junction in front of the imposing Gaumont cinema. After closure as a cinema in the 1970s it became a bingo hall and recently has received planning permission for conversion into a mosque. (B.R.Cox)

8. Clarence Pier

81.   No. 244 is about to depart on a short working of route 8 to Copnor Bridge in the summer of 1961. The newly rebuilt Clarence Pier can be seen to the left, and on the right are the newly opened Seahorse Bars, in front of which can be seen the rear of a Crossley waiting to depart on route 20 to Cosham. (B.R.Cox coll.)

82.   In this view, no. 250 is waiting to depart on route 8 to Green Lane, in the summer of 1961. We know that it is the summer (apart from the number of people about) because the crew in the centre of the view are wearing white hat covers and summer uniform. (B.R.Cox coll.)

9. Floating Bridge

83.   Views of trolleybuses on the High Street/Floating Bridge section of the trolleybus system are rare. This shot of no. 231 on the original route 16 from Floating Bridge to Copnor Bridge was taken in about 1950. It is waiting to depart from the Broad Street terminus in front of another World War II bomb site. This route was abandoned on 29th September 1951. (R.Marshall)

84.   This extremely rare pre-war shot shows no. 290 carrying out the reversing manoeuvre at the Floating Bridge terminus of the original routes 15-16. The arrangement used was followed at the Madeira Road terminus for Green Lane services constructed in 1952. (G.A.Tucker)

10. South Parade Pier to Dockyard via Palmerston Road

85.   This August 1934 view of no. 8, a Karrier with English Electric bodywork, is unusual because it appears to show the vehicle parked not at the specially constructed terminus for the trolleybuses at South Parade Pier, but at the point where Corporation motorbuses used to terminate. Possibly the new terminus was not completed when this shot was taken. This view is also unique in that it shows a Portsdown & Horndean Light Railway tram on the left of the picture at the company's South Parade Pier terminus. (T.Dethridge coll.)

86.   This 1950s view again clearly shows South Parade Pier terminus. Interestingly, it also appears to be used on this occasion as the terminus of the Southdown route 45A to Fareham. Behind the sign showing clearly that this was a private road can be seen Canoe Lake. (T.Dethridge coll.)

87.   An early post - war view features no. 280 at the South Parade Pier terminus. The conductor appears to be removing the bamboo pole prior to sorting out the dewired trolley poles. (T.Dethridge coll.)

88.   This 1937 view of an almost new no. 279 clearly shows the layout of the specially constructed road forming the South Parade Pier terminus for the trolleybuses. (T.Dethridge coll.)

90.   A mid-1950s view of no. 248 outside the Savoy Café and Ballroom, about to turn into Clarendon Road. (T.Dethridge coll.)

89.   This 1934 or 1935 view, taken at the newly-opened South Parade Pier trolleybus terminus, shows no. 9, also a Karrier with English Electric bodywork, at the terminus operating on route 3-4. Behind it can be seen no. 1, an AEC with English Electric bodywork. (T.Dethridge coll.)

91.   A crowd seems to have gathered on the promenade to witness the mishap which seems to have befallen no. 265 at the junction with Clarendon Road. The conductor is attempting to rewire the vehicle – not an easy task because trolley poles were set in contact with the overhead wires under tension provided by the large springs at the base of the poles. (T.Dethridge Coll)

92.   This 1961 view was taken at the end of Clarendon Road where it meets The Strand. No. 288   is seen here turning off The Strand into Waverley Road on route 8 to Green Lane. Campions, who ran the shop on the corner, were well-known bakers in Portsmouth. (B.R.Cox)

93.   This fascinating view of Handleys Corner, Palmerston Road, dates from 1947. The Craven-bodied AEC trolleybus is on route 8 & 9 or the original route 5, all of which served Palmerston Road at this time. The bomb-damaged site of Handleys was turned into an ornamental garden until rebuilding could begin in 1950. (A. Triggs)

94.   No. 270 is seen in 1961 travelling along Western Parade approaching the turning into Osborne Road. The tramlines still remain in situ along this stretch of road some 25 years after the trams were withdrawn! The building on the left in the background was the birthplace of Peter Sellers, the well-known actor. (B.R.Cox)

95.   Moving on towards the destination at the Dockyard, this photo shows no. 315 at Cambridge Junction. Portsmouth Grammar School is on the right on the corner of High Street, along which the original 15-16 service travelled to reach the Floating Bridge terminus until withdrawn in 1951. (B.R.Cox)

96.   This view was taken on a wet Wednesday evening in June 1963. The BUT Burlingham can be seen against the backdrop of the former Portsmouth Power Station, with its massive chimneys, which was demolished in the 1980s. Immediately on the right can be seen the wall surrounding HMS Vernon – now the Gunwharf Quays development. (B.R.Cox)

97.   This 1962 picture shows a Burlingham en route to South Parade Pier at the junction of Gunwharf Road with Park Road on the right. On the left behind the trees is the main entrance to the former HMS Vernon, now the Gunwharf Quays development. The view is dominated by the construction of the 20-storey Mill Gate House off St George's Square. (B.R.Cox)

98.   This was taken in November 1961 shortly before route 12 was converted to motorbus operation. No. 273 is under the railway bridge leading in Portsmouth Harbour Station. The advertisement for Pompey shows fixtures against Third Division opponents and also an interesting 'friendly' against Belgrade Sports Club. (B.R.Cox)

99.   No. 252 is seen at the Dockyard terminus on route 17 shortly after the end of World War II. Note the Nissen hut café next to the less than prestigious temporary premises of the gentlemen's outfitters, Moss Bros. (T.Dethridge coll.)

100.   This pre-war view shows an interesting line-up of vehicles at the Dockyard terminus looking towards the Dockyard Main Gate. Also visible in the foreground are the former tramlines which had been covered by the time this photograph was taken. (T.Dethridge coll.)

101. This panorama of the Dockyard terminus was taken in the summer of 1961 and shows a line-up abreast of nos. 255, 269 and 315, looking almost as if they are on parade, on three different trolleybus routes which terminated at the Dockyard at that time. (B.R.Cox)

1963

Corporation Trolley Bus Service 17

DOCKYARD — EASTNEY — MILTON — DOCKYARD

Via Guildhall, Bradford Junction, Albert Road, Highland Road, Milton, Goldsmith Avenue, Fratton Bridge, Bradford Junction, Guildhall.

Corporation Trolley Bus Service 17

WEEKDAY SERVICE

					NS		NS		NS		NS		NS		NS		NS				
Dockyard *Main Gate*	...	...	...	...	...	...	...	5 59	...	6 9	...	6 19	6 24	6 29	6 34	6 39	...	6 47	6‡52	6 58	7‡ 4
Guildhall	...	...	...	...	...	...	...	6 4	...	6 14	...	6 24	6 29	6 34	6 39	6 44	...	6 52	6‡57	7 3	7‡ 9
Bradford Junction ...	...	...	...	...	...	...	...	6 8	...	6 18	...	6 28	6 33	6 38	6 43	6 48	...	6 56	7‡ 1	7 7	7‡13
Festing Hotel ...	...	...	...	...	...	...	...	6 14	...	6 24	...	6 34	6 39	6 44	6 49	6 54	...	7 2	7‡ 7	7 13	7‡19
Eastney	5 0	5 24	5 39	5 54	6 3	6 8	6 13	6 18	6 23	6 28	6 33	6 38	6 43	6 48	6 53	6 58	7 3	7 6	7 11	7 17	7 23
Milton *White House* ...	5 2	5 26	5 41	5 56	6 5	6 10	6 15	6 20	6 25	6 30	6 35	6 40	6 45	6 50	6 55	7 0	7 5	7 8	7 13	7 19	7 25
Bradford Junction ...	5 8	5 32	5 47	6 2	6 11	6 16	6 21	6 26	6 31	6 36	6 41	6 46	6 51	6 56	7 1	7 6	7 11	7 14	7 19	7 25	7 31
Guildhall	5 12	5 36	5 51	6 6	6 15	6 20	6 25	6 30	6 35	6 40	6 45	6 50	6 55	7 0	7 5	7 10	7 15	7 18	7 23	7 29	7 35
Dockyard *Main Gate*	...	...	5 56	6 11	6 20	6 25	6 30	6 35	6 40	6 45	6 50	6 55	7 0	7 5	7 10	7 15	7 20	7 23	...	7 34	...

Dockyard *Main Gate*	7 10	7‡16	7 22	7‡28	7 34	7 46	7 58	8 10	8 22	8 34	8 46	8 58		10	22	34	46	58		6 10	6 22
Guildhall	7 15	7‡21	7 27	7‡33	7 39	7 51	8 3	8 15	8 27	8 39	8 51	9 3		15	27	39	51	3		6 15	6 27
Bradford Junction ...	7 19	7‡25	7 31	7‡37	7 43	7 55	8 7	8 19	8 31	8 43	8 55	9 7	and at the	19	31	43	55	7		6 19	6 31
Festing Hotel ...	7 25	7‡31	7 37	7‡43	7 49	8 1	8 13	8 25	8 37	8 49	9 1	9 13	following	25	37	49	1	13		6 25	6 37
Eastney	7 29	7 35	7 41	7 47	7 53	8 5	8 17	8 29	8 41	8 53	9 5	9 17	mins. past	29	41	53	5	17	until	6 29	6 41
Milton *White House* ...	7 31	7 37	7 43	7 49	7 55	8 7	8 19	8 31	8 43	8 55	9 7	9 19	each hour	31	43	55	7	19		6 31	6 43
Bradford Junction ...	7 37	7 43	7 49	7 55	8 1	8 13	8 25	8 37	8 49	9 1	9 13	9 25		37	49	1	13	25		6 37	6 49
Guildhall	7 41	7 47	7 53	7 59	8 5	8 17	8 29	8 41	8 53	9 5	9 17	9 29		41	53	5	17	29		6 41	6 53
Dockyard *Main Gate*	7 46	...	7 58	...	8 10	8 22	8 34	8 46	8 58	9 10	9 22	9 34		46	58	10	22	34		6 46	6 58

Dockyard *Main Gate*	6 34	6 46	6 58	7 11	7 26	7 41	7 56		11	26	41	56		1011	1026	1041	1056	1111	1122	1137
Guildhall	6 39	6 51	7 3	7 16	7 31	7 46	8 1		16	31	46	1		1016	1031	1046	11 1	1116	1127	113
Bradford Junction ...	6 43	6 55	7 7	7 20	7 35	7 50	8 5	then at the	20	35	50	5		1020	1035	1050	11 5	1120	1131	114
Festing Hotel ...	6 49	7 1	7 13	7 26	7 41	7 56	8 11	following	26	41	56	11		1026	1041	1056	1111	1126	1137	114
Eastney	6 53	7 5	7 17	7 30	7 45	8 0	8 15	mins. past	30	45	0	15	until	1030	1045	11 0	1115	1130	1141	115
Milton *White House* ...	6 55	7 7	7 19	7 32	7 47	8 2	8 17	each hour	32	47	2	17		1032	1047	11 2	...	...	...	...
Bradford Junction ...	7 1	7 13	7 25	7 38	7 53	8 8	8 23		38	53	8	23		1038	1053	11 8	...	...	...	...
Guildhall	7 5	7 17	7 29	7 42	7 57	8 12	8 27		42	57	12	27		1042	1057	1112	...	...	...	...
Dockyard *Main Gate*	7 10	7 22	7 34	7 47	8 2	8 17	8 32		47	2	17	32		1047	11 2	1117	...	...	...	...

11. Rolling Stock

FLEET LIST 1934 - 1963

1 – 4   Chassis: AEC 661T, built 1934
Body: English Electric H50R
Equipment: English Electric

   1 † RV 4649
   2   RV 4650
   3   RV 4651
   4   RV 4652

Renumbered 201-204 in 1938. Trolleybus 4 (204) decorated for the Coronations in 1937 and 1953

   † Preserved by Portsmouth City Museums

5 – 7   Chassis: Leyland TBD2, built 1934
Body: English Electric H50R
Equipment: General Electric Company

   5   RV 4653
   6   RV 4654
   7   RV 4655

Renumbered 205-207 in 1938

8   Chassis: Karrier E4, built 1934
Body: English Electric H50R
Equipment: British Thompson Houston

   8   RV 4656

Renumbered 208 in 1938

9   Chassis: Karrier E4, built 1934
Body: English Electric H50R
Equipment: English Electric

   9   RV 4657

Renumbered 209 in 1938

10   Chassis: Sunbeam MF2, built 1934
Body: Metro-Cammell H50R
Equipment: British Thompson Houston

   10   RV 4660

Renumbered 210 in 1938

11   Chassis: Karrier E4, built 1934
Body: Metro-Cammell H50R
Equipment: British Thompson Houston

   11   RV 4661

Renumbered 211 in 1938

12   Chassis: AEC 661T, built 1934
Body: English Electric H60R
Equipment: English Electric

   12   RV 4658

Renumbered 212 in 1938

This vehicle was loaned to Pontypridd UDC during the war. On return to Eastney, remained in store until its disposal in January 1954.

13   Chassis: Sunbeam MS3, built 1934
Body: English Electric H60R
Equipment: British Thompson Houston

   13   RV 4659

Renumbered 213 in 1938 and loaned to Pontypridd UDC during the war.

14   Chassis: Sunbeam MS3, built 1934
Body: Metro-Cammell H60R
Equipment: British Thompson Houston

   14   RV 4662

Renumbered 214 in 1938 and loaned to Pontypridd UDC during the war.

15   Chassis: AEC 663T, built 1934
Body: Metro-Cammell H60R
Equipment: English Electric

   15   RV 4663

Renumbered 215 in 1938 and loaned to Pontypridd UDC during the war.

16-24   Chassis: AEC 661T, built 1935/6
Body: English Electric H50R
Equipment: English Electric

       RV 6374 - 6382

Renumbered 216 to 224 in 1938.

25-54   Chassis: AEC 661T, built 1936
Body: Craven H26/26R
Equipment: English Electric

       RV 8307 - 8336

Renumbered 225 to 254 in 1938

55 – 100   Chassis: AEC 661T, built 1936/7
Body: Craven H26/26R
Equipment: English Electric

       RV 9106 – 9145
          and
       RV 9149 – 9154

Renumbered 255 to 300 in 1938

301 - 315   Chassis: BUT 9611T, built 1950/1
Body: Burlingham H28/24R
Equipment: English Electric

       ERV 926 – 940

Trolleybus 303 withdrawn in 1961 as a result of an accident at Milton, and the rest withdrawn upon the abandonment of the trolleybus system. Trolleybus 313 is known to be preserved.

102.   No. 10, a Sunbeam MF2 with Metro-Cammell bodywork, is seen here on test in Wolverhampton prior to delivery in July 1934. It first entered service end of August 1934 and was withdrawn in 1953. Sunbeam was a subsidiary of Guy Motors whose vehicles were manufactured in Wolverhampton. (T.Dethridge coll.)

103.   Nos. 16, 19 and 18 were AECs with English Electric bodywork and are seen here on test on AEC's test circuit in Southall prior to delivery in 1935. They first entered service in November 1935 and were withdrawn in 1955/1957. (T.Dethridge coll.)

104.   No. 24 AEC had English Electric bodywork and is seen prior to delivery. It first entered service in April 1936 and was withdrawn in October 1958. Note the 'streamlined' encasing around the base of the trolley booms – the only Portsmouth trolleybus to receive this treatment. (T.Dethridge coll.)

105.   No. 25, an AEC with Craven bodywork, is seen here at Craven's Sheffield works prior to delivery. It first entered service in August 1936 and was withdrawn in June 1959. (T.Dethridge coll.)

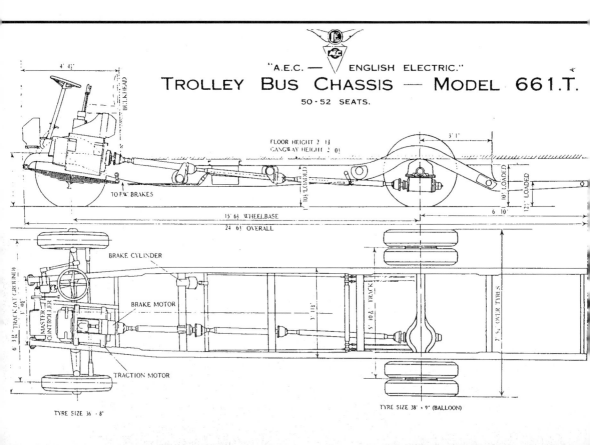

"A.E.C. — ENGLISH ELECTRIC."

TROLLEY BUS CHASSIS — MODEL 661.T.

50·52 SEATS.

106.   This unique view shows a chassis of one of the AEC trolleybuses forming part of the 16-24 batch delivered in 1935/6. It is seen at AEC's Southall works. (T.Dethridge coll.)

107.   Nos. 204 and 205 are seen at Cosham Compound in the late 1940s. No. 204 is an AEC with English Electric bodywork and no. 205 is a Leyland also with English Electric bodywork. Both entered service in August 1934 and were withdrawn in 1955 and 1953 respectively. (W.J.Haynes)

108. No. 215 was an AEC 6-wheeler with Metro-Cammell bodywork and is looking immaculate after having just left the paint shop in 1949. This vehicle had been leant to Pontypridd UDC from 1942-1946. It first entered service in July 1934 and was withdrawn in 1953. (T.Dethridge coll.)

109. No. 225 (formerly no. 25) is seen opposite Eastney Depot fresh from the paint shop in the early 1950s (see also photograph no. 105). (B.R.Cox coll.)

110. The elegant lines of the Burlingham bodywork, which was unique to the Portsmouth system, are shown to full effect in this view of no. 308 in 1952, shortly after it entered service. (E.Surfleet)

111.   No. 204 was decorated for the coronation of King George VI in 1937. (B.R.Cox coll.)

112.   No. 204 again, decorated this time advertising King George's Fund in May 1945. (B.R.Cox coll.)

113.   Yes, no. 204 yet again – this time decorated for the coronation of Queen Elizabeth II and seen here at the Copnor Bridge end of New Road. (B.R.Cox coll.)

CITY OF PORTSMOUTH PASSENGER TRANSPORT DEPARTMENT.

RETURN OF THE KING and QUEEN FROM SOUTH AFRICA. May 12th, 1947.

The Bearer is a School Child and is permitted to travel free of charge on any public service of the Portsmouth Passenger Transport Department in going between his home and the United Services Recreation Ground between the hours of 8 a.m. and 1 p.m. on Monday, May 12th, 1947.

B. HALL,
General Manager and Engineer

114.   No. 303 is seen after having come to grief in Milton Road in April 1961. Six passengers were injured after the collision with a trolley standard. This was one of only two major trolleybus accidents throughout the entire operation of the Portsmouth system. (B.R.Cox)

115.   One of the two Dennis tower wagons was recorded shortly after the war at North End junction. Both vehicles had been converted in 1933 and provided sterling service throughout the war until they were withdrawn and replaced by the Leyland TD2s in 1952. (G.A.Tucker)

116.   Leyland TD2 tower wagon no. TW1 is seen shortly after its conversion from bus no. 17 in 1952. It remained in service until 1963 and is now preserved (B.R.Cox Coll)

117.   The last trolleybus on route 18 was no. 301, seen here entering Eastney Depot on 27th July 1963. Although the 17-18 route had been converted to motorbuses some five weeks earlier, the last workings to Eastney each day were by trolleybuses which had operated the last journeys on the 5-6 route to the Dockyard. (A.R.Cox)

118.   The actual last trolleybus to arrive at Eastney was no. 313 on route 17, seen here after arrival at the Depot with a commemorative notice in the upper nearside front window. Surprisingly perhaps, there was no formal civic ceremony to mark the occasion. (A.R.Cox)

119.   After withdrawal of the trolleybuses, some were acquired for breaking by a scrap dealer in Bedhampton. No. 249 is seen here awaiting its fate. (B.R.Cox)

120.   This final view of several of the Cravens in an advanced state of being dismantled provides an excellent illustration of their wooden-framed bodies. The rear lower destination screen seems to have remained in place, perhaps in a last defiant gesture? (B.R.Cox)

Middleton Press

Easebourne Lane, Midhurst, W Sussex. GU29 9AZ Tel: 01730 813169 Fax: 01730 812601
*If books are not available from your local transport stockist, order direct with cheque,
Visa or Mastercard, post free UK.*

BRANCH LINES
Branch Line to Allhallows
Branch Line to Alton
Branch Lines around Ascot
Branch Line to Ashburton
Branch Lines around Bodmin
Branch Line to Bude
Branch Lines around Canterbury
Branch Lines around Chard & Yeovil
Branch Line to Cheddar
Branch Lines around Cromer
Branch Lines to East Grinstead
Branch Lines of East London
Branch Lines to Effingham Junction
Branch Lines around Exmouth
Branch Lines to Falmouth, Helston & St. Ives
Branch Line to Fairford
Branch Lines around Gosport
Branch Line to Hayling
Branch Lines to Henley, Windsor & Marlow
Branch Line to Hawkhurst
Branch Lines around Huntingdon
Branch Line to Ilfracombe
Branch Line to Kingswear
Branch Line to Lambourn
Branch Lines to Launceston & Princetown
Branch Line to Looe
Branch Line to Lyme Regis
Branch Lines around Midhurst
Branch Line to Minehead
Branch Line to Moretonhampstead
Branch Lines to Newport
Branch Lines to Newquay
Branch Lines around North Woolwich
Branch Line to Padstow
Branch Lines around Plymouth
Branch Lines to Seaton and Sidmouth
Branch Lines around Sheerness
Branch Line to Shrewsbury
Branch Line to Swanage *updated*
Branch Line to Tenterden
Branch Lines around Tiverton
Branch Lines to Torrington
Branch Line to Upwell
Branch Lines of West London
Branch Lines around Weymouth
Branch Lines around Wimborne
Branch Lines around Wisbech

NARROW GAUGE
Branch Line to Lynton
Branch Lines around Portmadoc 1923-46
Branch Lines around Porthmadog 1954-94
Branch Line to Southwold
Douglas to Port Erin
Douglas to Peel
Kent Narrow Gauge
Northern France Narrow Gauge
Romneyrail
Southern France Narrow Gauge
Sussex Narrow Gauge
Two-Foot Gauge Survivors
Vivarais Narrow Gauge

SOUTH COAST RAILWAYS
Ashford to Dover
Bournemouth to Weymouth
Brighton to Worthing
Eastbourne to Hastings
Hastings to Ashford
Portsmouth to Southampton
Ryde to Ventnor
Southampton to Bournemouth

SOUTHERN MAIN LINES
Basingstoke to Salisbury
Bromley South to Rochester
Crawley to Littlehampton
Dartford to Sittingbourne
East Croydon to Three Bridges
Epsom to Horsham
Exeter to Barnstaple
Exeter to Tavistock
Faversham to Dover
London Bridge to East Croydon
Orpington to Tonbridge
Tonbridge to Hastings
Salisbury to Yeovil
Sittingbourne to Ramsgate
Swanley to Ashford
Tavistock to Plymouth
Three Bridges to Brighton
Victoria to Bromley South
Victoria to East Croydon
Waterloo to Windsor
Waterloo to Woking
Woking to Portsmouth
Woking to Southampton
Yeovil to Exeter

EASTERN MAIN LINES
Barking to Southend
Ely to Kings Lynn
Ely to Norwich
Fenchurch Street to Barking
Ipswich to Saxmundham
Liverpool Street to Ilford
Saxmundham to Yarmouth
Tilbury Loop

WESTERN MAIN LINES
Didcot to Swindon
Ealing to Slough
Exeter to Newton Abbot
Newton Abbot to Plymouth
Newbury to Westbury
Paddington to Ealing
Paddington to Princes Risborough
Plymouth to St. Austell
Princes Risborough to Banbury
Reading to Didcot
Slough to Newbury
St. Austell to Penzance
Taunton to Exeter
Westbury to Taunton

MIDLAND MAIN LINES
Euston to Harrow & Wealdstone
St. Pancras to St. Albans

COUNTRY RAILWAY ROUTES
Abergavenny to Merthyr
Andover to Southampton
Bath to Evercreech Junction
Bournemouth to Evercreech Junction
Burnham to Evercreech Junction
Cheltenham to Andover
Croydon to East Grinstead
Didcot to Winchester
East Kent Light Railway
Fareham to Salisbury
Guildford to Redhill
Reading to Basingstoke
Reading to Guildford
Redhill to Ashford
Salisbury to Westbury
Stratford upon Avon to Cheltenham
Strood to Paddock Wood
Taunton to Barnstaple
Wenford Bridge to Fowey
Westbury to Bath
Woking to Alton
Yeovil to Dorchester

GREAT RAILWAY ERAS
Ashford from Steam to Eurostar
Clapham Junction 50 years of change
Festiniog in the Fifties
Festiniog in the Sixties
Festiniog 50 years of enterprise
Isle of Wight Lines 50 years of change
Railways to Victory 1944-46
Return to Blaenau 1970-82
SECR Centenary album
Talyllyn 50 years of change
Yeovil 50 years of change

LONDON SUBURBAN RAILWAYS
Caterham and Tattenham Corner
Charing Cross to Dartford
Clapham Jn. to Beckenham Jn.
Crystal Palace (HL) & Catford Loop
East London Line
Finsbury Park to Alexandra Palace
Holbourn Viaduct to Lewisham
Kingston and Hounslow Loops
Lewisham to Dartford
Lines around Wimbledon
London Bridge to Addiscombe
Mitcham Junction Lines
North London Line
South London Line
West Croydon to Epsom
West London Line
Willesden Junction to Richmond
Wimbledon to Beckenham
Wimbledon to Epsom

STEAMING THROUGH
Steaming through Cornwall
Steaming through the Isle of Wight
Steaming through Kent
Steaming through West Hants
Steaming through West Sussex

TRAMWAY CLASSICS
Aldgate & Stepney Tramways
Barnet & Finchley Tramways
Bath Tramways
Brighton's Tramways
Bristol's Tramways
Burton & Ashby Tramways
Camberwell & W.Norwood Tramways
Clapham & Streatham Tramways
Croydon's Tramways
Dover's Tramways
East Ham & West Ham Tramways
Edgware and Willesden Tramways
Eltham & Woolwich Tramways
Embankment & Waterloo Tramways
Enfield & Wood Green Tramways
Exeter & Taunton Tramways
Greenwich & Dartford Tramways
Hammersmith & Hounslow Tramways
Hampstead & Highgate Tramways
Hastings Tramways
Holborn & Finsbury Tramways
Ilford & Barking Tramways
Kingston & Wimbledon Tramways
Lewisham & Catford Tramways
Liverpool Tramways 1. Eastern Routes
Liverpool Tramways 2. Southern Routes
Liverpool Tramways 3. Northern Routes
Maidstone & Chatham Tramways
Margate to Ramsgate
North Kent Tramways
Norwich Tramways
Reading Tramways
Seaton & Eastbourne Tramways
Shepherds Bush & Uxbridge Tramways
Southend-on-sea Tramways
Southwark & Deptford Tramways
Stamford Hill Tramways
Twickenham & Kingston Tramways
Victoria & Lambeth Tramways
Waltham Cross & Edmonton Tramways
Walthamstow & Leyton Tramways
Wandsworth & Battersea Tramways

TROLLEYBUS CLASSICS
Croydon Trolleybuses
Derby Trolleybuses
Hastings Trolleybuses
Huddersfield Trolleybuses
Maidstone Trolleybuses
Portsmouth Trolleybuses
Woolwich & Dartford Trolleybuses

WATERWAY ALBUMS
Kent and East Sussex Waterways
London to Portsmouth Waterway
West Sussex Waterways

MILITARY BOOKS
Battle over Portsmouth
Battle over Sussex 1940
Bombers over Sussex 1943-45
Bognor at War
Military Defence of West Sussex
Military Signals from the South Coast
Secret Sussex Resistance
Surrey Home Guard

OTHER RAILWAY BOOKS
Index to all Middleton Press stations
Industrial Railways of the South-East
South Eastern & Chatham Railways
London Chatham & Dover Railway
War on the Line (SR 1939-45)

BIOGRAPHY
Garraway Father & Son